Portals

At the intersection of landscape and self

by Beth Thompson

with selections from William Bartram's *Travels* (1791)

Table of Contents

Portals to Plants

Portals to Waters

Preface to Portals

Portals book and card deck intend to explore the intersection of landscape and self. Why explore the intersection of landscape and self? Do the self and landscape intersect? I would argue that each of us intersects with the land, knowingly or not, when we take a bite of food or a sip of water. To become aware of the landscape we inhabit, and how that landscape impacts our day-to-day existence, is to embark on a journey of discovery. It is my hope that wherever you reside you will become more attuned to the landscape that surrounds you. You may find yourself in relationship with the birdsong, rainfall, sunlight, moonlight, waters and earth, buildings and creatures in your landscape as you move through this book and card deck.

Travels

This world, as a glorious apartment of the boundless palace of the sovereign Creator, is furnished with an infinite variety of animated scenes, inexpressibly beautiful and pleasing, equally free to the inspection and enjoyment of all his creatures.

Perhaps there is not any part of creation, within the reach of our observations, which exhibits a more glorious display of the Almighty hand, than the vegetable world. Such a variety of pleasing scenes, ever changing, throughout the seasons, arising from various causes and assigned each to the purpose and use determined.

~ *William Bartram,* Travels, *p. xiv.*

Portals begins with William Bartram's ethereal descriptions from *Travels through North & South Carolina, Georgia, East & West Florida, the Cherokee Country, the Extensive Territories of the Muscogulges, or Creek Confederacy, and the Country of the Chactaws* (1791). I began to work with Bartram's words in 2012. I chose Bartram because he defines the ecological past of the landscape of the Southeastern United States where I reside, write, and photograph. His writings, which I quote in this book with original spellings and punctuation, give a sense of the grandeur of the landscape, something easily missed as we speed past forgotten groves at 70 mph. Bartram's writings ask that we slow down. Keen observation of the environment helps us arrive at the crossroad of landscape and self. Knowing from whence we came is key to way-finding.

Photographs

However, it is not enough to simply know what was. We also need to know what is. Thus the second portal into the intersections of landscape and self provided is a photographic portal. These portals illustrate, emphasize, and visualize each intersection in the book, showing both the changes in our environment and the resilience of the land. There are 12 photographs in the categories of cities, creatures, plants and waters, for a mesh of 48 crossroads to explore.

Questions for Contemplation

Now that we have seen the ecological past through Bartram's words, and a snapshot of today's environment, how does this Southeastern Landscape intersect with the deeper self? Questions for Contemplation provide a portal for exploration within. The questions may be answered with writing, drawing, painting, collaging, photographing, meditation, or movement. Strike a pose that encapsulates the question, then move into a pose that answers it. Use the question as a prompt to inspire poetry. Gather with friends, and have a group collaging session, each person using one question as a prompt, then share your creations with one another. Take a walk through the landscape with the echo of Bartram's words and your camera or sketchbook in hand. Or find your own way to explore the intersection of self and landscape.

Possible Perceptions

Lastly, I have provided a portal into the world through artwork I call Possible Perceptions. Created from a single triangle taken from the photograph accompaniment replicated repeatedly, Possible Perceptions mimic fractal geometry. Fractal geometry is a pattern that is self-similar at all scales. Fractal geometry describes the simple beauty of the unfurling of a fern in springtime. Fractals also describe the complexity of a long-leaf pine ecosystem and the kaleidoscope of creatures that depend upon it and how they rely on one another. So Possible Perceptions embody complexity, a complexity that arises from simple repetition. For me Possible Perceptions visually represent systems. In a system, the whole is greater than its parts. Thus these kaleidoscopic Possible Perceptions attempt to illustrate the enormity of the connection between landscape and self.

Welcome

It is thus that I invite you to enter Portals, to a world revolving around art, poetry, photography, history and herstory, literature and contemplation. May you find inspiration here. May you find solace here. May you find yourself here. May you find wonder here. May you find hope here. Welcome to Portals.

Portals to Cities

1. Charleston, SC

At the request of Dr. Fothergill, of London, to search the Floridas, and the western parts of Carolina and Georgia, for the discovery of rare and useful productions of nature, chiefly in the vegetable kingdom; in April, 1773, I embarked for Charleston, South-Carolina, on board the brigantine Charleston Packet....

William Bartram, *Travels*, p. 1.

William Bartram had a clear purpose for his *Travels* - to discover rare and useful productions of nature, in particular, plants. In *Portals,* my purpose is to connect inner knowing with outer beauty, providing a contemplative journey home. The journey begins deep in the Southeastern United States. Viewed through the lens of William Bartram's *Travels*, then my photography, the trip culminates in questions for contemplation and is punctuated by possible perceptions.

What is my purpose?

What are my strengths?

What resources does the Universe provide me?

Because all I need is provided, I will embark upon...

Ravenel Bridge, Charleston, SC

Opposite Page: Charleston Bridge Possible Perception

2. Dillard Road

After passing through this meadow, the road led me over the bases of a ridge of hills, which as a bold promontory dividing the fields I had just passed, form expansive green lawns. On these towering hills appeared the ruins of the ancient famous town of Sticoe. Here was a vast Indian mount or tumulus and great terrace, on which stood the council-house, with banks encompassing their circus; here were also old Peach and Plumb orchards....

William Bartram, *Travels*, p. 345.

Dillard Road, NC-GA Line

Where might I be led?

What kind of road am I on? A well-traveled interstate, a city street crowded with stop lights, an empty country road...

What does this road or path I have chosen say about me?

If I could choose a road to travel, I would...

Opposite Page:
Road To Highlands Possible Perception

3. Fort Frederica, GA

Frederica was the first town built by the English in Georgia, and was founded by General Oglethorp, who began and established the colony. The fortress was regular and beautiful, constructed chiefly with brick, and was the largest, most regular, and perhaps most costly, of any in North America, of British construction: it is now in ruins, yet occupied by a small garrison; the ruins also of the town only remain....

William Bartram, *Travels*, p. 62.

Fort Frederica, St. Simons Island, GA

Giving my troubles to the wind...

I visited Fort Frederica, located on the river and marshes. A storm was blowing up, and the wind was strong and steady, so I gave my troubles to the wind, imagining them being blown away.

What ruins do I wish to visit?

Who occupies my fortress?

If the wind gently blew all my troubles away, I would...

Opposite Page:
Fort Frederica Possible Perception

4. Savannah, GA Rainstorm

O peaceful Alatamaha! gentle by nature! how thou art ruffled! ....The tempest now relaxes.... The waters are purified, the waves subside, and the beautiful river regains its native calmness: so it is with the...human events on the stream of life...the most painful feelings are excited in the mind when...some unforeseen accident intervenes, and surprises us;... every idea of happiness recedes; the splendour of glory darkens, and at length totally disappears; every pleasing object is defaced, all is deranged...we are apt to deviate from...virtue, to shut our eyes upon our guide and protector, doubt of his power..... But let us wait and rely on our God, who...will shine forth in brightness...and reveal to us how finite ...is human power, when assuming...wisdom.

William Bartram, *Travels*, pp. 51~52.

Storm, Savannah, GA
Opposite Page:
Storm Possible Perception

When do I get ruffled on the stream of life?

When do I forget to rely upon Source Energy?

What do I learn from these struggles?

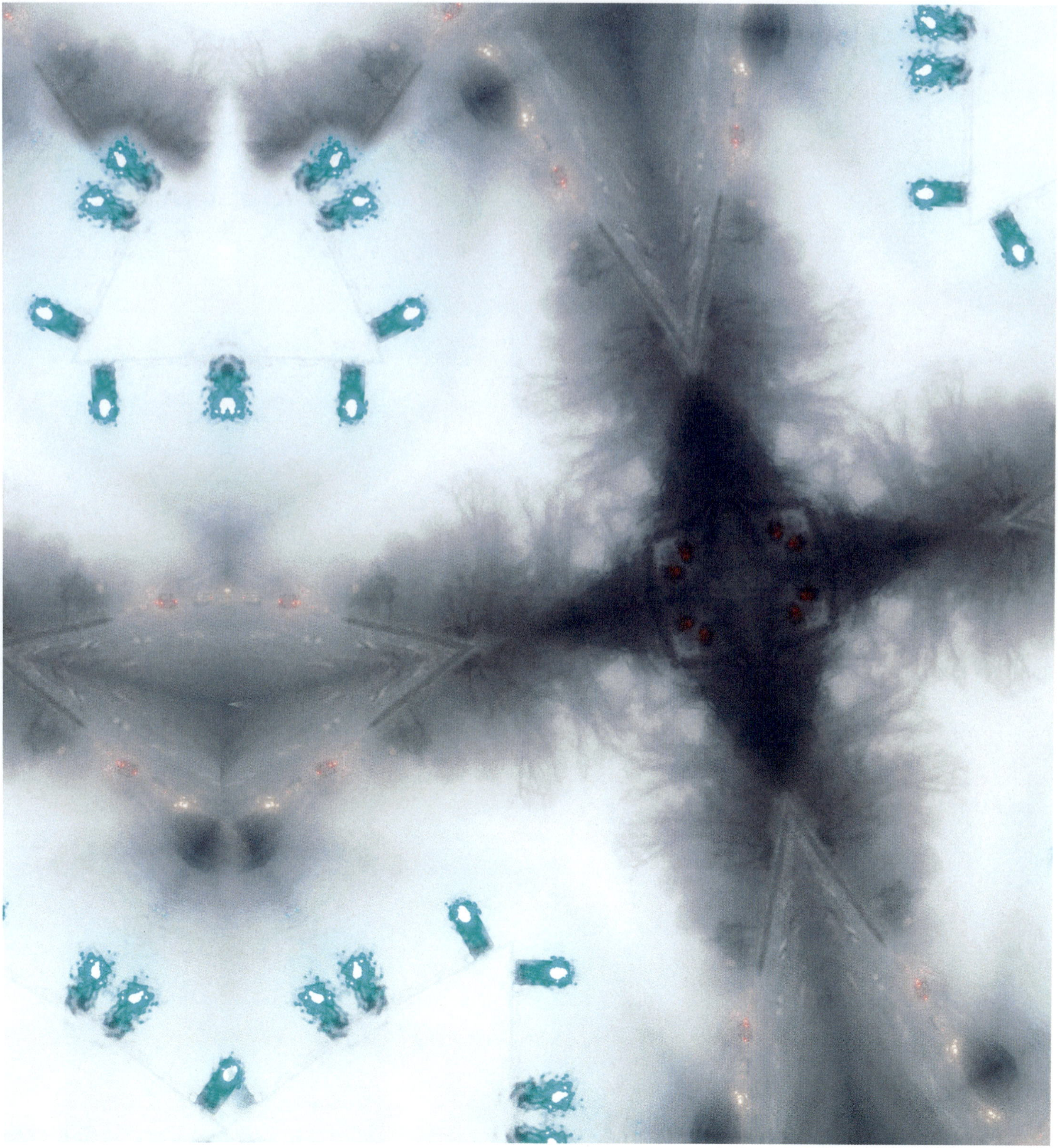

5. Tunnel in Mobile, AL

... burning flies tormenting our horses to such a degree, as to excite compassion even in the hearts of pack-horsemen.... we travelled ...amidst a flying host of these persecuting spirits, who formed a vast cloud around our caravan so thick as to obscure every distant object...the leading horses were continually in a gore of blood....[The flies] are armed with a strong sharp beak... making a large orifice from whence the blood springs in large drops, rolling down as tears....almost sinking under the persecutions from the evil spirits...we halted at noon....

William Bartram, *Travels*, pp. 384~386.

The benefit of exoskeletons...

My speed, in the neighborhood of 70 to 80 miles per hour, out-distanced the lowly mosquito by about 66 times. The dreaded horsefly would still out-distance me, flying at a speed of 90 miles per hour. Thanks, however, to my handy-dandy Volkswagen exoskeleton of plastic, glass, and steel, the horsefly did not plague me on my journey to Alabama.

Bankhead Tunnel, Mobile, AL
Opposite Page: Tunnel Possible Perception

In what ways do I stand on the shoulders of giants?

What benefits of the modern world do I take for granted?

What do I do that would not be possible without those who have gone before me?

6. Fort Toulouse, AL

The trader obliged me...on a visit to the Alabama, an Indian town at the confluence of the two fine rivers, the Tallapoose and Coosau, which here resign their names to the great Alabama, where are to be seen traces of the ancient French fortress, Thoulouse....one of the most elegible situations for a city in the world, a level plain between the conflux of two majestic rivers...each navigable for vessels and perreauguas at least five hundred miles above it...many hundred miles before we reach their sources in the Apalachean mountains.

William Bartram, *Travels*, p. 447.

Three Rivers, Fort Toulouse, AL

Opposite Page: Three Rivers Possible Perception

William felt that this confluence would be one of the most eligible situations for a city in the world, yet Montgomery grew up some miles south on the Alabama River. This left the Indian mound to become overgrown, remnants of Ft. Thoulouse to survive to the present day, and the area around the confluence of two rivers to remain parkland.

What rivers of energy are converging in my world?

7. Mobile, AL

The city of Mobile is situated on the easy ascent of a rising bank, extending near half a mile back on the level plain above; it has been near a mile in length, though now chiefly in ruins, many houses vacant and mouldering to earth....

The fort Conde, which stands very near the bay, towards the lower end of the town is a large regular fortress of brick.

The principal French buildings are constructed of brick....

William Bartram, *Travels*, p. 403.

Vines on Brick Wall, Mobile, AL

What do my bricks contain?

A fortress? A house? A building?

What is the purpose of the structures in my life, both physical and figurative?

Are the containers in my life fulfilling a need or constraining me?

Opposite Page: Mobile Possible Perception

8. Ocmulgee Mounds, GA

The pyramidal hills or...mounts and highways, or avenues, leading from them to...lakes or ponds, vast tetragon terraces, chunk yards and obelisks or pillars of wood, are the only monuments of labour, ingenuity and magnificence, that I have seen worthy of notice, or remark...mounts, with spacious and extensive avenues, leading from them out of the town, to an artificial lake or pond of water...monuments of magnificence, to perpetuate the power and grandeur of the nation...they exhibit scenes of power...and must have been public edifices.

William Bartram, *Travels*, pp. 520~521.

Ocmulgee Mounds, Macon, GA

What monuments of magnificence do I take for granted today?

How do I acknowledge the monuments of magnificence in my life?

What would happen if I saw the labor, ingenuity, and magnificence all around me?

How can I celebrate the grandeur of my nation?

Opposite Page:
Container of the Sun Possible Perception

9. Buffalo Lick, GA

After four days moderate and pleasant travelling, we arrived in the evening at the Buffalo Lick....The place called the Lick contains three or four acres....The earth...is an almost white or cinerious coloured tenacious fattish clay, which...cattle lick into great caves, pursuing the delicious vein. It is the common opinion of the inhabitants, that this clay is impregnated with saline vapours... but I could discover nothing saline in its taste, but I imagined an insipid sweetness. Horned cattle, horses, and deer, are immoderately fond of it....

William Bartram, *Travels*, p. 39.

Possible Site of Buffalo Lick, Temperance Bell, GA
Opposite Page: Buffalo Lick Possible Perception

Did the Buffalo change the earth at Buffalo Lick?

When I trust change, I ....

What are my responses to foundational change?

10. Cowford, FL

In three days after leaving Amelia, we arrived at the Cow-ford, a public ferry, over St. Johns, about thirty miles above the bar or capes, the river here being above a mile wide.

William Bartram, *Travels*, p. 71.

St. Johns River, Jacksonville, FL

Opposite Page: Jacksonville Possible Perception

The public ferry at Cow-Ford became Jacksonville, FL, in the time since William traveled there.

What cow-fords grew into great cities of experience?

Where are my rivers of energy most navigable?

How has my river of energy changed over time?

Do I wish to ford this river or build on its banks?

11. Metropolis of Georgia

The Savanna uninterruptedly flows with a gentle meandring course, and is navigable...to Savanna, where ships of three hundred tons lie in a capacious and secure harbour. Augusta thus seated at the head of navigation...commands the trade and commerce of vast fruitful regions above it...will very soon become the metropolis of Georgia.

William Bartram, *Travels*, p. 317.

Augusta, GA, Spring 2014

Opposite Page: Metropolis of Georgia Possible Perception

Augusta became the capital of Georgia for a time, before it was surplanted by the railroad and Atlanta.

What is the capital city of my being made of?

How do I resonate with rivers, railroads, and highways?

How has a metropolis influenced me?

Has one metropolis of experience been supplanted by another?

12. Cowee Vale, NC

...Here terminates the great vale of Cowe, exhibiting one of the most charming natural mountainous landscapes perhaps any where to be seen; ridges of hills rising grand and sublimely one above and beyond another, some boldly and majestically advancing into the verdant plain, their feet bathed with the silver flood of the Tanase, whilst others far distant, veiled in blue mists, sublimely mount aloft, with yet greater majesty lift up their pompous crests and overlook vast regions.

The vale is closed at Cowe by a ridge of mighty hills, called the Jore mountain, said to be the highest land in the Cherokee country, which crosses the Tanase here.

William Bartram, *Travels*, pp. 352~353.

Atop Cowee Mound, Cowee, NC

Opposite Page: Cowee Vale Possible Perception

Cowee has been returned to the Cherokee People. On my visit we climbed the mound in wonder. We couldn't see the village, or the people, or the sacredness of the mound. Climbing down into the woods: a boulder with holes from years of women's labor grinding corn kernels and acorns. Suddenly becoming alive: the village, its people, the sacredness of the mound.

What makes sacred space alive to me?

Portals to Creatures

13. Spanish Curlews

It is a pleasing sight at times of high winds and heavy thunder storms, to observe the numerous squadrons of these Spanish curlews driving to and fro, turning and tacking about, high up in the air, when by their various evolutions in the different and opposite currents of the wind high in the clouds, their silvery white plumage gleams and sparkles like the brightest chrystal, reflecting the sun-beams that dart upon them between the dark clouds.

William Bartram, *Travels*, p. 149.

Spanish Curlews, Okefenokee Swamp, GA
Opposite page: Bright Squadrons Possible Perception

What sunbeams dart upon me?

How do I feel watching a flock of birds soar before a storm?

How do I cope with various evolutions in different and opposite currents of the wind?

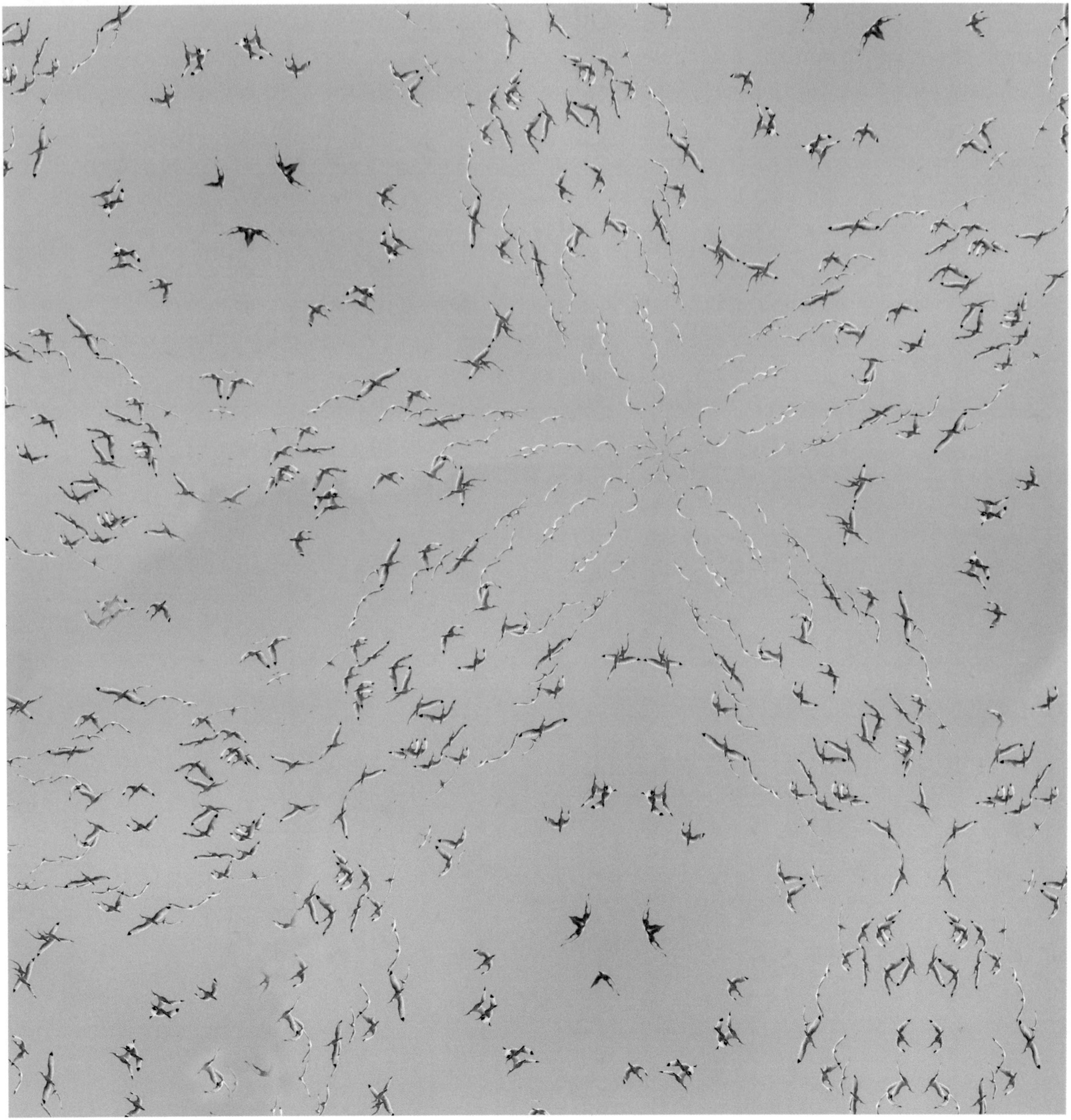

14. Salt Springs Fish

But behold yet something far more admirable, see whole armies descending into an abyss, into the mouth of the bubbling fountain, they disappear! are they gone forever? is it real? I raise my eyes with terror and astonishment,--I look down again to the fountain with anxiety, when behold them as it were emerging from the blue ether of another world, apparently at a vast distance, at their first appearance, no bigger than flies or minnows, now gradually enlarging, their brilliant colours begin to paint the fluid.

Now they come forward rapidly, and instantly emerge, with the elastic expanding column of chrystaline waters, into the circular bason or funnel, see now how gently they rise, some upright, others obliquely, or seem to lay as it were on their sides, suffering themselves to be gently lifted or born up, by the expanding fluid towards the surface, sailing or floating like butterflies in the cerulean ether: then again they as gently descend, diverge and move off; when they rally, form again and rejoin their kindred tribes.

William Bartram, *Travels*, p. 166.

Salt Springs Fish, Salt Springs, FL
Opposite page: Salt Springs Fish Possible Perception

What cycles in and out of an abyss in my life?

How can a fish be like a butterfly?

What comes to me through cerulean ether?

Who is in your kindred tribe?

15. Carrion Crows

...the coped vulture...by the inhabitants called the carrion crow....His wings are...broad and round at their extremities, having a clumsy appearance; the tail is remarkably short, which he spreads like a little fan, when on the wing; they have a heavy laborious flight, flapping their wings, then sail a little and then flap their wings again, and so on as if recovering themselves when falling; the beak is very long and strait, until it makes a sudden hook at the point....

William Bartram, *Travels*, p. 152.

Vulture Tree, St. John's Riverbank, FL
Opposite page: Sky Kings Possible Perception

I cannot be graceful and accomplished in every part of my life.

When is my flight heavy and laborious?

What are the areas where I am clumsy?

How can I let my clumsiness be ok with me?

16. Alligator

...the young are not left to shift for themselves, having had frequent opportunities of seeing the female alligator, leading about the shores her train of young ones, just like a hen does her brood of chickens, and she is equally assiduous and courageous in defending the young, which are under their care, and providing for their subsistence; and when [s]he is basking upon the warm banks, with her brood around her, you may hear the young ones continually whining and barking, like young puppies.

William Bartram, *Travels*, p. 128.

Baby alligator, St. Johns River, FL

How do you defend
your inner child?

How can being
assiduous and courageous be
a way of caring?

Imagine being under the
care of a fierce creature such as
a female alligator...

Opposite page: Alligator Possible Perception

17. Sea Cows

...the manate or sea cow, in the winter season; part of a skeleton of one, which the Indians had killed last winter, lay upon the banks of the spring; the grinding teeth were about an inch in diameter; the ribs eighteen inches in length, and two inches and an half in thickness, bending with a gentle curve, this bone is esteemed equal to ivory; the flesh of this creature is counted wholesome and pleasant food; the Indians call them by a name which signifies the big beaver. ...they feed chiefly on aquatic grass and weeds.

William Bartram, *Travels*, pp. 231~232.

Manatee, Blue Springs, FL

Without the manatee eating grass and weeds, would the waterways become clogged and impassable?

If I valued
my teeth and bones
the way the world values ivory,
what might I change in how I care for them?

How can I express my own
wholesomeness and pleasantness?

Opposite page: Manatee Possible Perception

18. Snake Birds

Here is in this river and in the waters all over Florida, a...bird, the people call them Snake Birds...I have seen paintings of them on the Chinese screens.... The head and neck of this bird are extremely small and slender... all the upper side, the abdomen and thighs, are as black and glossy as a raven's, covered with feathers so firm and elastic, that they in some degree resemble fish-scales, the breast and upper part of the belly are covered with feathers of a cream colour,...they behold their images in the watery mirror: ...they drop off the limbs into the water as if dead... [then] their long slender head and neck only appear, and have very much the appearance of a snake....

William Bartram, *Travels*, pp. 132~133.

Snake Bird, St. John's Riverbank, FL
Opposite page: Snake Bird Possible Perception

How am I one thing but appear like another?

In what areas of my life do I engage in black-and-white thinking, failing to see the whole bird?

What images do you behold in the watery mirror?

19. Bee and Spider

...I was greatly surprised at the sudden appearance of a remarkable large spider...I soon noticed that the object of his wishes was a large fat bomble bee... that was visiting the flowers...this cunning intripid hunter...advancing with slow steps obliquely, or under cover of dense foliage, and behind the limbs, and when the bee was engaged in probing a flower he would leap nearer, and then instantly retire out of sight, under a leaf or behind a branch...when he had now got within two feet of his prey, and the bee was intent on sipping the delicious nectar from a flower...he instantly sprang upon him, and grasped him over the back and shoulder,when for some moments they both disappeared, I expected the bee had carried of[f] his enemy, but to my surprise they both together rebounded back again, suspended at the extremity of a strong [e]lastic thread or web, which the spider had artfully let fall...the rapidity of the bee's wings, endeavouring to extricate him-self, made them both together appear as a moving vapor, until the bee became fatigued by whirling round, first one way and then back again; at length, in about a quarter of an hour, the bee quite exhausted by his struggles, and the repeated wounds of the butcher, became motionless, and quickly expired in the arms of the devouring spider, who, ascending the rope with his game, retired to feast on it... and perhaps before night became himself, the delicious evening repast of a bird or lizard.

William Bartram, *Travels*, pp. xxix~xxxi

Bee and Spider
Opposite page: Bee and Spider Possible Perception

Am I the bee or the spider?

What do I hunt for?

What repast nourishes me?

20. Gopher Tortoise

Observed as we passed over the sand hills, the dens of the great land tortoise, called gopher: this strange creature remains yet undescribed by historians and traveller....They are to be seen only on the high dry sand hills. When arrived to their greatest magnitude, the upper shell is near eighteen inches in length, and ten or twelve inches in breadth; the back is very high....The fore part of the belly shell towards its extremity, is formed somewhat like a spade....

....the general colour of the animal is a light ash or clay, and at a distance, unless he is in motion, any one would disregard or overlook it as a stone or an old stump. It is astonishing what a weight one of these creatures will bear; it will easily carry any man standing on its back....

William Bartram, *Travels*, pp. 182~183.

Gopher Tortoise, Albany Zoo, Georgia
Opposite page: Gopher Possible Perception

Where am I camouflaged by my coloring?

What weight do I bear?

What weights do I choose to bear?

21. Turning Over

I never before this was afraid at the sight of an Indian, but at this time, I must own that my spirits were very much agitated: I saw at once, that being unarmed, I was in his power, and having now but a few moments to prepare, I resigned myself entirely to the will of the Almighty, trusting to his mercies for my preservation; my mind then became tranquil, and I resolved to meet the dreaded foe with resolution and chearful confidence.

William Bartram, *Travels*, p. 21.

Sea Turtle Greeting
Opposite page: Sea Turtle Possible Perception

How can I surrender to the waves of life?

Today, I let go of....

If I were to let go, then I would....

22. Great Blue Heron

These floating islands present a very entertaining prospect; for although we behold an assemblage of the primary productions of nature only, yet the imagination seems to remain in suspence and doubt; as in order to enliven the delusion and form a most picturesque appearance, we see not only flowery plants, clumps of shrubs, old weather-beaten trees, hoary and barbed, with the long moss waving from their snags, but we also see them compleatly inhabited, and alive, with crocodiles, serpents, frogs, otters, crows, herons, curlews, jackdaws, &c.

William Bartram, *Travels*, pp. 89~90.

Great Blue Heron, St. John's River, FL
Opposite page: Great Blue Possible Perception

How do I enliven my delusions to form a picturesque appearance?

Am I completely inhabited and alive, or is there space, a void, in my life?

Can I be as still as this Great Blue Heron?

23. Indigo Snake

There is another snake in Carolina and Florida...which is a very beautiful creature, and I believe not of a distructive or vindictive nature; these when grown...are about five feet in length, and near as thick as a man's arm; their skin scaly but smooth and shining, of a pale grey and sky colour ground, uniformly marked with transverse undulatory ringlets or blotches of a deep nut brown, edged with red or bright Spanish brown; they appear innocent, very active and swift, endeavouring to escape from one; they have no poisonous fangs.

William Bartram, *Travels*, p. 273.

Bartram did not describe the Indigo Snake in* Travels, *hence this excerpt on the Milk Snake.

Indigo Snake, Bear Hollow Zoo, Athens, GA
Opposite page: Indigo Snake Possible Perception

What species other than my own do I depend on for life?

The Indigo Snake is one of over 300 species whose life depends on the gopher tortoise.

What is my nature? What is not my nature?

24. Bear and Squirrel

...the hunter fired, and laid the largest [bear] dead on the spot, ... when presently the other [bear]...approached the dead body, smelled, and pawed it, and appearing in agony, fell to weeping and looking upwards, then towards us, and cried out like a child. Whilst our boat approached very near, the hunter was loading his rifle in order to shoot the survivor, which was a young cub, and the slain supposed to be the dam; the continual cries of this afflicted child, bereft of its parent, affected me very sensibly, I was moved with compassion, and charging myself as if accessary to what now appeared to be a cruel murder, and endeavoured to prevail on the hunter to save its life, but to no effect! for by habit he had become insensible to compassion towards the brute creation, being now within a few yards of the harmless devoted victim, he fired, and laid it dead, upon the body of the dam.

William Bartram, *Travels*, pp. xxvi~xxvii.

Bear and Squirrel,
Bear Hollow Zoo, Athens, GA
Opposite page: Bear and Squirrel
Possible Perception

How do I express compassion to the bears in my life?

Where have I become insensible to compassion by habit?

When am I the hunter? the observer? the bear?

Portals to Plants

25. Reaching Hands

What power or faculty is it, that directs the ... climbers, towards the twigs of shrubs, trees and other friendly support? we see them invariably leaning, extending and like the [f]ingers of the human hand, reaching to catch hold of what is nearest, just as if they had eyes to see with, and when their hold is fixed, to coil the tendril in a spiral form, by which artifice it becomes more elastic and effectual...

...is it sense or instinct that influences their actions? it must be some impulse; or does the hand of the Almighty act and perform this work in our [s]ight?

William Bartram, *Travels*, p. xxi.

Vine, Panther Creek Trail, Clarkesville, GA

Let's do the locomotion...

A vine growing on the tree doesn't tell the tree how tall to grow, and the tree doesn't tell the vine how often to wrap itself around its trunk, how high to reach. Similarly, the Universe may have given me gifts, yet how I use those gifts is up to me.

Am I the tree or the vine?

How do vines add curves and spirals to my life?

How may I curve to be more elastic and effective?

What gifts from the Universe am I using today?

Opposite Page:

Panther Creek Trail Possible Perception

26. Sarracenia

...what a quantity of water a leaf is capable of containing, about a pint! Taste of it--how cool and animating--limpid as the morning dew: nature seems to have furnished them with this cordated appendage or lid, which turns over, to prevent a too sudden, and copious supply of water from heavy showers of rain....whether the insects caught in their leaves, and which dissolve and mix with the fluid, serve for aliment or support to these kind of plants, is doubtful.

William Bartram, *Travels*, pp. xviii~xx.

Pitcher Plant, Okefenokee Swamp, GA

Taste of it–how cool and animating–limpid as the morning dew...

That William drank the water caught in the pitcher plant–this is what stands out to me.

What serves as aliment and support for me?

What supports me in this moment?

What in me needs to dissolve and mix to give me strength?

Opposite Page:
Pitcher Plant Possible Perception

27. Spicy Groves

Our rural table was spread under the shadow of Oaks, Palms, and Sweet Bays, fanned by the lively salubrious breezes wafted from the spicy groves. ...the brilliant humming-bird darted through the flowery groves, suspended in air, and drank nectar from the yellow Jasmine, Lonicera, Andromeda, and sweet Azalea.

William Bartram, *Travels*, p. 61.

I can communicate many things remotely to you. Words, ideas, theories. Adventures. Stories. Pictures. Visual Fine Art. The sound of William's words, rhythm, cadence. Songs. But those most primal senses, taste, touch, sadly I cannot bottle up and send to you. For the scent of jasmine in full blossom on a warm humid evening, you will simply have to travel to the jasmine to experience its fragrance.

What spicy groves are sacred to me?

Where do I find delight in the senses of scent and taste?

Where do I find a connection to the primal?

Backyard Jasmine, Athens, GA

Opposite Page: Jasmine Possible Perception

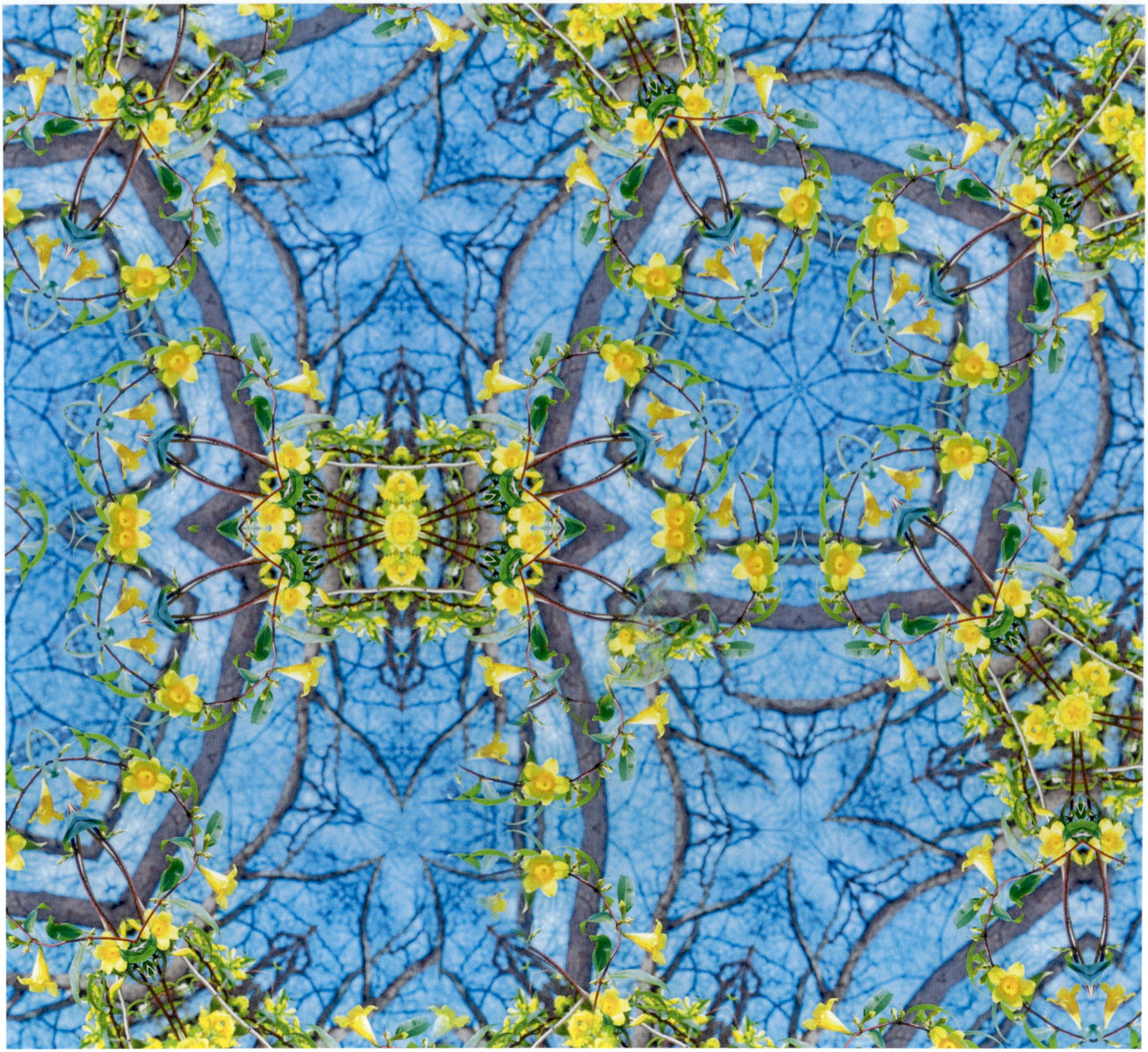

28. Blossoming Magnolia

The Laurel Magnolia, which grows on this river are the most beautiful and tall, that I have any where seen, unless we except those, which stand on the banks of the Missisippi; yet even these must yield, to those of St. Juan, in neatness of form, beauty of foliage, and I think, in largeness and fragrance of flower.

William Bartram, *Travels*, pp. 85~86.

Beneath the Magnolia,
North Campus, UGA, Athens, GA

Sheltering Magnolias...

The stately magnolias that William Bartram so loved still grow abundantly in the Southeast. I cannot count the times that William Bartram sheltered beneath a magnolia tree on his travels throughout the Southeast. He mentions camping beneath them many times in his book, *Travels*.

Where is your place of refuge?

What shelters you?

Does that tree or place have a special scent?

List some of your favorite scents and your memories associated with them.

Opposite Page: Magnolia Cathedral Window

29. Iris

At this time the town was fasting, taking medicine, and I think I may say praying, to avert a grevious calamity of sickness...taking at the same time by way of medicine or physic, a strong decoction of the roots of the Iris versicolor, which is a powerful cathartic;... every town cultivates ... it having a large artificial pond, just without the town, planted and almost overgrown with it... I observed where they had lately been digging up this root.

William Bartram, *Travels*, pp. 455~456.

Iris, Augusta, South Carolina side
Opposite Page: Iris Possible Perception

We have forgotten the use of the root of the Iris, now that it is grown as a decorative plant. But once it was cathartic, releasing that which was pent up, healing, and saving lives.

What in your life has a forgotten function?

What have you pent up?

What would happen if the blockages released?

30. Paw Paw Tree

...Annona.... The leaves are long, extremely narrow, almost lineal....The flowers, both in size and colour, resemble those of the Antrilobe, and are single from the axillae of the leaves on incurved pedunculi, nodding downwards. I never saw the fruit.

William Bartram, *Travels*, p. 18.

Paw Paw Blossom, Bartram's Garden, Philadelphia, PA
Opposite Page: Paw Paw Possible Perception

The Paw Paw is pollinated by flies, then makes an edible fruit similar to the banana.

What blooms in your life?

What pollination do these blossoms need to become edible fruits?

Where do you need pollination, mixing, blending, or tempering?

31. Long Leaf Dawn

Behold how gracious and beneficent smiles the roseate morn! now the sun arises and fills the plains with light, his glories appear on the forests, encompassing the meadows, and gild the top of the terebinthine Pine...

William Bartram, *Travels*, p. 245.

Long Leaf Pine at Dawn, Seminole State Park, GA
Opposite Page: Long Leaf Dawn Possible Perception

Waking before dawn at Seminole State Park, I watched as the sun came up over the horizon. The tops of Bartram's terebinthine pines, standing tall, were the first to catch the sun's rays. Thus I experienced the same gilding of the pines that Bartram spoke of centuries ago!

What light rises in your life to gild your trees with gold?

What time of day am I most productive?

What time am I most social?

Spend a week noticing your own circadian rhythm.

32. The Divine Monitor Within

We are, all of us, subject to crosses and disappointments, but more especially the traveller; and when they surprise us, we frequently become restless and impatient under them: but let us rely on Providence, and by studying and contemplating the works and power of the Creator, learn wisdom and understanding in the economy of nature, and be seriously attentive to the divine monitor within. Let us be obedient to the ruling powers in such things as regard human affairs, our duties to each other, and all creatures and concerns that are submitted to our care and controul.

William Bartram, *Travels*, p. 57.

Fort Frederica Orange Tree

I too am subject to crosses and disappointments. I carried a cross with me down South.

Giving it to the wind...
I visited Fort Frederica, located on the river and marshes. A storm was blowing up, and the wind was strong and steady, so I gave my troubles to the wind, imagining them being blown away. On my way back up to Savannah, after leaving the wind and the sea behind, finally I became attentive to

the Divine Monitor Within...
Around Fort Frederica, all of Saint Simons flourishes, but Frederica quietly sits, bearing oranges.

How can I be more attentive to the Divine Monitor Within?

What natural economies do I encourage?

How do I turn over my cares to the Divine Monitor?

Opposite Page: Orange Tree Possible Perception

33. Live Oak

The trunk of the Live Oak is generally from twelve to eighteen feet in girt, and rises ten or twelve feet erect from the earth...then divides itself into three, four, or five great limbs, which...grow in nearly an horizontal direction, each limb forming a gentle curve, or arch, from its base to its extremity. I... stepped...fifty paces...from the trunk of one of these trees, to the extremity of the limbs.

William Bartram, *Travels*, pp. 84~85.

Live Oak,Skidaway Island, GA

Live Oaks are regal:

Quercus sempervirens,
an evergreen oak tree growing in the southern-most portions of the United States. Draped with streamers of the Spanish moss, or limbs covered with the green fur of resurrection fern, the Native people made acorn oil from their nuts.

Like the Oaks, which can only bear 3 to 5 great limbs, our human energies are also finite. Sometimes it helps me to identify what branches of my life are most important to me today.

Among the branches of my life, I choose...

What does my life tree support or bear?

If I were simply a streamer of Spanish moss, floating on a limb, then I would...

Opposite Page: Live Oak Possible Perception

34. *Arundo gigantea*

*And as a proof of the extraordinary fertility of the soil, the reeds or canes (*Arundo gigantea*) grow here thirty or forty feet high, and as thick as a man's arm, or three or four inches in diameter; I suppose one joint of some of them would contain above a quart of water, and these reeds serve very well for setting poles, or masts for barks and canoes.*

William Bartram, *Travels*, p. 410.

River Cane, Cherokee, NC

Opposite Page: River Cane Possible Perception

River Cane

River Cane reminds me of what has been lost or permanently altered in the Southeastern landscape. Replaced by the invasive species of bamboo, much as the Native people who still weave river cane baskets were replaced by invasive Europeans. Yet River Cane survives today...

What has been altered by time but not extinguished in me?

What can I weave with the river cane in my life?

35. Bottlebrush Buckeye

This plain is mostly a forest of the great long-leaved pine....the earth covered with grass, interspersed with an infinite variety of herbacious plants, and embellished with extensive savannas, always green, sparkling with ponds of water, and ornamented with clumps of evergreen, and other trees and shrubs, as Magnolia grandiflora...[and] Fothergilla....

William Bartram, *Travels*, pp. 30~31.

Bottlebrush Buckeye, Athens, GA
Opposite Page: Bottlebrush Buckeye Possible Perception

Fothergilla

Named for Bartram's benefactor, John Fothergill, red bottlebrush buckeye is a favorite of hummingbirds in the spring. Later in the summer it forms a buckeye, considered lucky by some.

What am I attracting with my nectar?

Am I a plain, a pond, or a savannah?

How do I wish to ornament myself?

What spring blossoms are bearing fall harvest for me?

36. *Franklinia Alatmaha*

...the flowers are very large, expand themselves perfectly, are of a snow-white colour, and ornamented with a crown or tassel of gold coloured refulgent staminae in their centre... the borders of the petals are crisped or plicated: these large, white flowers stand single and sessile in the bosom of the leaves which...make a gay appearance....We never saw it grow in any other place, nor have I ever since seen it growing wild, in all my travels....

William Bartram, *Travels*, pp. 467~468.

Franklinia Blossom, Clayton, GA
Opposite Page: Franklinia Close-Up Possible Perception

Unlike my species, which is on the verge of overpopulating the planet, *Franklinia alatmaha* is extinct in the wild. Collected by John and William Bartram, it has survived total extinction. Today a single tree produces more fruit than a single human can study.

What paradoxes are present in me today?

How can limitations also set me free?

What do I wish to cultivate so that it can thrive?

Portals to Waters

37. Stony Creek

In the evening we came to camp near the banks of Stony Creek, a large rapid water about six miles beyond the river. Next day we travelled about twenty miles farther, crossing two considerable creeks named Great and Little Tobosochte, and at evening encamped close by a beautiful large brook called Sweet Water, the glittering wavy flood passing along actively over a bed of pebbles and gravel.

William Bartram, *Travels*, pp. 381~382.

Creek at Ben Burton Park, Athens, GA

The Landscapes of Home:

The landscapes of my life I explore the most intimately: Hilly, above the fall line, with granite outcrops and boulders exposed, babbling brooks.

If your brook could speak, what would it say?

Describe an intimate landscape of your life.

What composes the bed of your glittering wavy flood? What are the banks containing?

Opposite Page: Stony Creek
Possible Perception

38. Falling Creek

...rushing from rocky precipices under the shade of the pensile hills, the unparalleled cascade of Falling Creek, rolling and leaping off the rocks...spread a broad, glittering sheet of chrystal waters, over a vast convex elivation of plain, smooth rocks, and are immediately received by a spacious bason, where, trembling in the centre through hurry and agitation, they gently subside, encircling the painted still verge, from whence gliding swiftly, they soon form a delightful little river, which continuing to flow more moderately, is restrained for a moment, gently undulating in a little lake, they then pass on rapidly to a high perpendicular steep of rocks, from whence these delightful waters are hurried down with irresistible rapidity.

William Bartram, *Travels*, p. 341.

What cascade of love is unparalleled in my life?

How can I roll and leap off the rocks in my path?

If my heart is a spacious basin, what emotions is it receiving today?

Describe an emotion I would like to rest in.

Describe an emotion I would like to hurry along with irresistible rapidity.

Dry Falls, Highlands, NC

Opposite Page: Dry Falls Possible Perception

39. April Creek

Thus secure and tranquil, and meditating on the marvellous scenes of primitive nature, as yet unmodified by the hand of man, I gently descended the peaceful stream, on whose polished surface were depicted the mutable shadows from its pensile banks; whilst myriads of finny inhabitants sported in its pellucid floods.

William Bartram, *Travels*, p. 49.

April Creek, Athens, GA

Opposite Page: April Creek Possible Perception

What streams tranquility into my world?

What streams security into my life?

How do I sport in the floods of my life?

How do I reflect mutable shadows today? How would I like to?

Name the inhabitants of my pellucid floods.

40. In Search of the Daughters of the Sun

The river St. Mary has its source from a vast lake, or marsh, called Ouaquaphenogaw... [The Creeks]...say it is inhabited by a peculiar race of Indians, whose women are incomparably beautiful; they also tell you, that [in] this terrestrial paradise...some of their enterprising hunters, when in pursuit of game, who being lost in inextricable swamps and bogs, and on the point of perishing, were unexpectedly relieved by a company of beautiful women, whom they call daughters of the sun, who kindly gave them such provisions as they had with them, which were chiefly fruit, oranges, dates, &c. and some corn cakes, and then enjoined them to fly for safety to their own country; for that their husbands were fierce men, and cruel to strangers....

William Bartram, *Travels*, pp. 24~25.

True Form of the Daughters of the Sun
Opposite Page: Daughters of the Sun Possible Perception

Where Bartram Never Traveled:

William actually never made it into the Okefenokee Swamp. Perhaps it is a good thing; had he entered the swamp, he might not have lived to write *Travels*. Recently, a guide decided to go to Bugaboo Island in the swamp. He hiked into Bugaboo Island from his campsite, bringing only a machete. He couldn't find his way back. Wandering for 5 days, eaten alive by mosquitoes, for relief he laid in shallow swamp water, thus only half his body was bitten. He would pass out and wake up to vultures, waiting for him to weaken. He was saved only because he saw a rescue helicopter land.

What thrives in the swamps of my soul?

What are my gatekeepers?

What bogs me down?

Where lies my promised land that I have yet to travel to?

41. Savannas

Drawing near the high shores, I ascended the steep banks, where stood a venerable oak.... It was nearly encircled with an open forest of stately pines (Pinus palustris) through which appears the extensive savanna, the secure range of the swift roebuck. In front of my landing, and due east, I had a fine prospect of the river and low lands on each side, which gradually widened to the sea coast, and gave me an unconfined prospect, whilst the far distant sea coast islands, like a coronet, limited the hoary horizon.

William Bartram, *Travels*, p. 50.

Marsh at Skidaway Island, Savannah, GA
Opposite Page: Savannah Possible Perception

What expands and deepens my sense of self?

The marshes of the Georgia seacoast expand and deepen my sense of self. Watching the tides fill them, then empty them, then fill them once again, I find myself in an endless flowing dance.

What fills you, empties you, and fills you again?

42. Foaming Surf

...our situation elevated and open, commanded a comprehensive landscape; the great ocean, the foaming surf breaking on the sandy beach, the snowy breakers on the bar, the endless chain of islands, checkered sound and high continent all appearing before us.

William Bartram, *Travels*, p. 268.

Seafoam at Hunting Island, SC
Opposite Page: Beach Reflections Possible Perception

The sandy beach is a demarcation between the ocean and the land. A between place. A place where a connection between land and sea is made.

Where are the connections, the between places, in your life?

What does my ocean bring me when it breaks on the sandy beaches of my continent?

From an elevated and open situation, what do I see?

Draw an ocean and fill it with connections to islands and continents, creatures, and waters that describe you or your life today.

43. Cypress Swamp

Upon doubling the point, I arrived at the landing, which is a circular harbour, at the foot of the bluff, the top of which is about twelve feet high; and back of it is a large Cypress swamp, that spreads each way, the right wing forming the West coast of the little lake, and the left stretching up the river many miles, and encompassing a vast space of low grassy marshes.

William Bartram, *Travels*, p. 116.

Cypress Swamp, Mobile, AL

The limbs of the cypress tree I photographed in the swamp spread out over the oily black water as if to reach out and grab passers-by. Perhaps the tree feels lonely and reaches out to find a friend. Perhaps the tree sees opportunity—growing on the edge of the swamp of cypress to take advantage of the sunlight over the water.

The water of the cypress swamp fascinates—so deep black and like a mirror reflecting all that comes its way, but concealing all that falls in. Cypress knees pierce the black surface, knees growing upwards while their reflection in the oily black water grows down into the swamp.

What grows in my spreading swamps?

When I am lonely, whom do I reach out to?

How am I an opportunist?

Where are the oily black places in me that reflect the light?

Opposite Page: Cypress Swamp Possible Perception

44. The Ocmulgee

After leaving the river we met with nothing material, or worth particular observation, until our arrival at Oakmulge, towards evening, where we encamped in expansive ancient Indian fields, in view of the foaming flood of the river, now raging over its banks.

William Bartram, *Travels*, p. 458.

Ocmulgee River, Juliette, GA
Opposite Page: Ocmulgee Possible Perception

When I photographed the Ocmulgee River in Juliette, GA, it was peaceful, reflecting the clouds and the sky.

What causes your river to rage over its banks?

What causes your river to foam in flood?

When is your river peaceful and reflective?

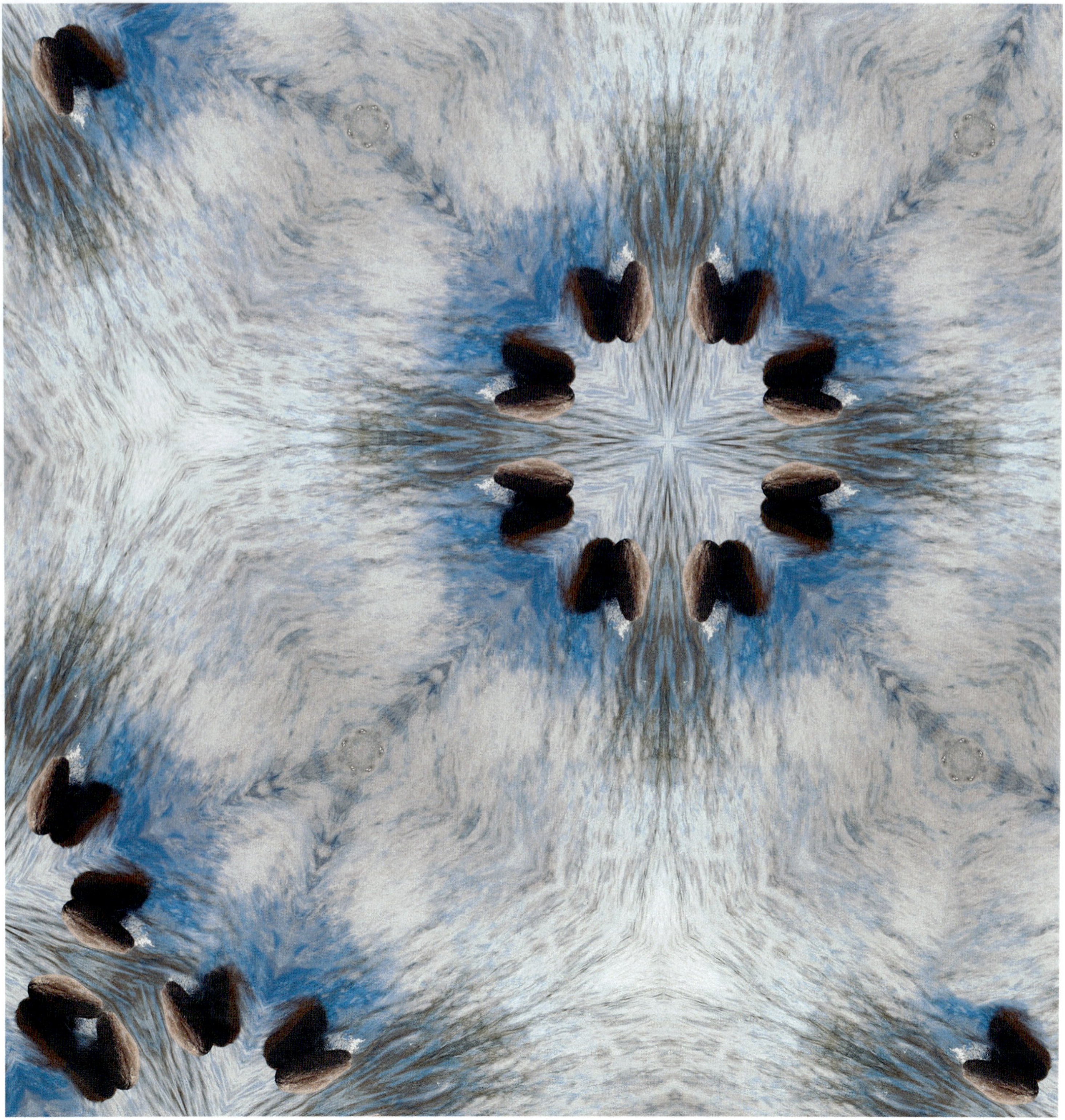

45. Billows and Breakers

...while I made a tour round the south point of the island, walking the shelly paved sea beach, and picking up novelties....I retired to a little distance, mounted the sand hills, and sat down, enjoying a fine prospect of the rolling billows and foaming breakers, beating on the bar, and north promontory of Amelia Isle, opposite to me.

William Bartram, *Travels*, p. 65.

Fort George's Sound, Nassau County, FL

What fine prospects do you enjoy at the beach?

What structures in your life afford you a view over your landscapes, like Bartram's sand hills?

What can you do to retire at a little distance from everyday life?

Opposite Page:
Driftwood Beach Possible Perception

46. Catawba River

...I now approach the river at the fording place, which was greatly swolen by the floods of rain that fell the day before, and ran with foaming rapidity, but observing that it had fell several feet perpendicular, and perceiving the bottom or bed of the river to be level, and covered evenly with pebbles, I ventured to cross over....

William Bartram, *Travels*, p. 347.

Catawba River, Morganton, NC

The rivers Bartram wrote of flow either to the Atlantic Ocean or the Gulf of Mexico. While he didn't visit the Catawba River in Morganton, NC, the Catawba flows to the Gulf, exhibiting a river bed covered evenly with pebbles.

Where are the fording places in your world?

What vast expanse of waters does your river empty into?

What does the bed or bottom of your river look like?

Opposite Page:
Catawba River Possible Perception

47. Savannah River

...from Augusta downwards to the ocean, a distance of near three hundred miles by water. The Savanna uninterruptedly flows with a gentle meandring course, and is navigable for vessels of twenty or thirty tons burthen to Savanna, where ships of three hundred tons lie in a capacious and secure harbour.

William Bartram, *Travels*, pp. 316~317.

Savannah River, Augusta, GA

What course does your river take?

Gentle and meandering?

Rapid and rocky?

Uninterrupted?

What ships navigate your river?

Is there a secure and capacious harbor for your river and its ships?

Opposite Page:
Savannah River Possible Perception

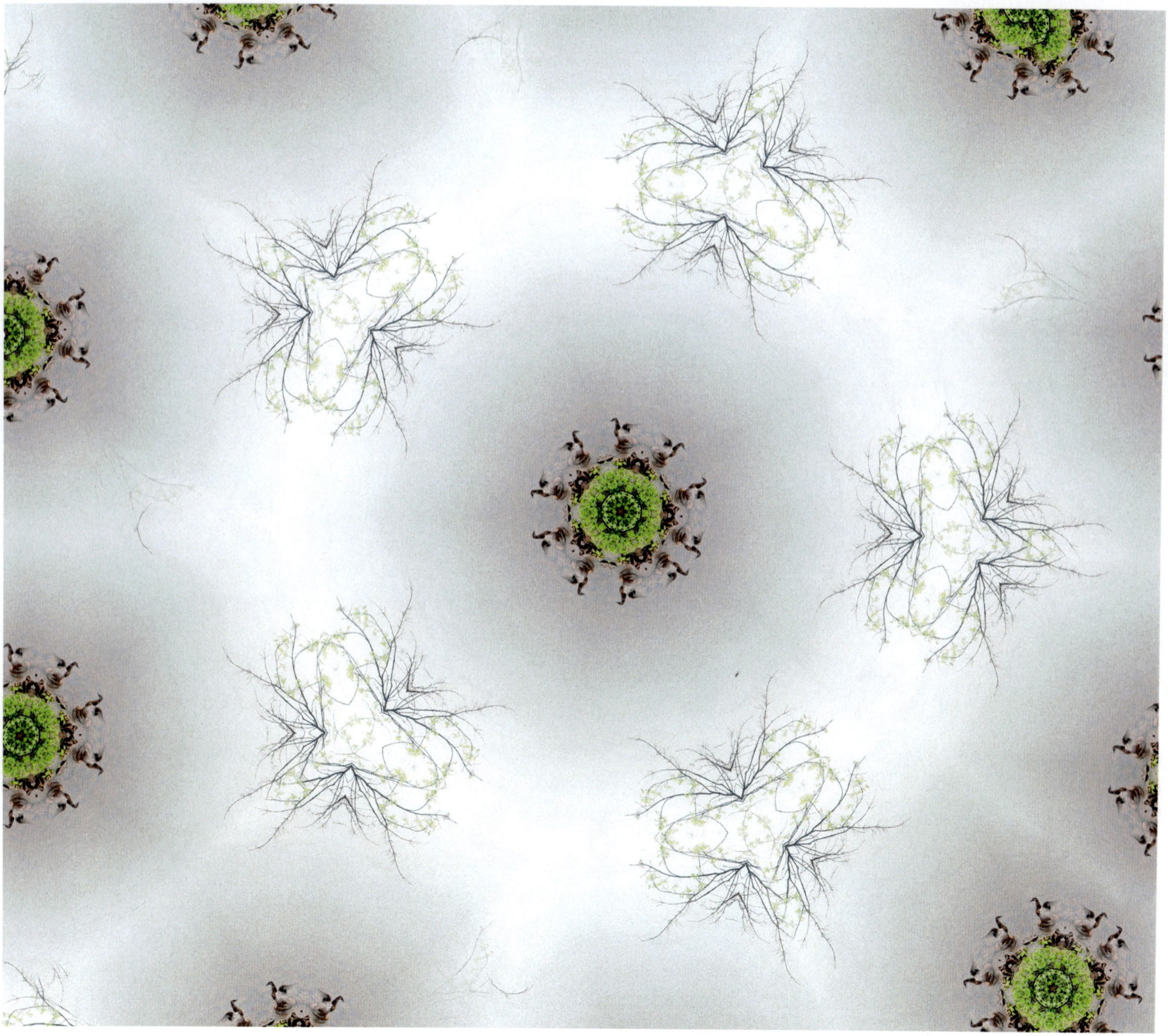

48. Oconee River

Our hunters going out, and, understanding that their route was to the low lands on the Ocone, I accompanied them: we had not rode above three miles before we came to the banks of that beautiful river.

William Bartram, *Travels*, pp. 42~43.

Oconee River, The Botanical Gardens of Georgia, Athens, GA

I spent my childhood in the Upper Oconee Watershed.

What watershed did you grow up in?

What river has low lands for you to visit?

What watershed do you live in now?

How would our society be different if we hailed from different watersheds instead of different cities and states?

Opposite Page:
Oconee River Possible Perception

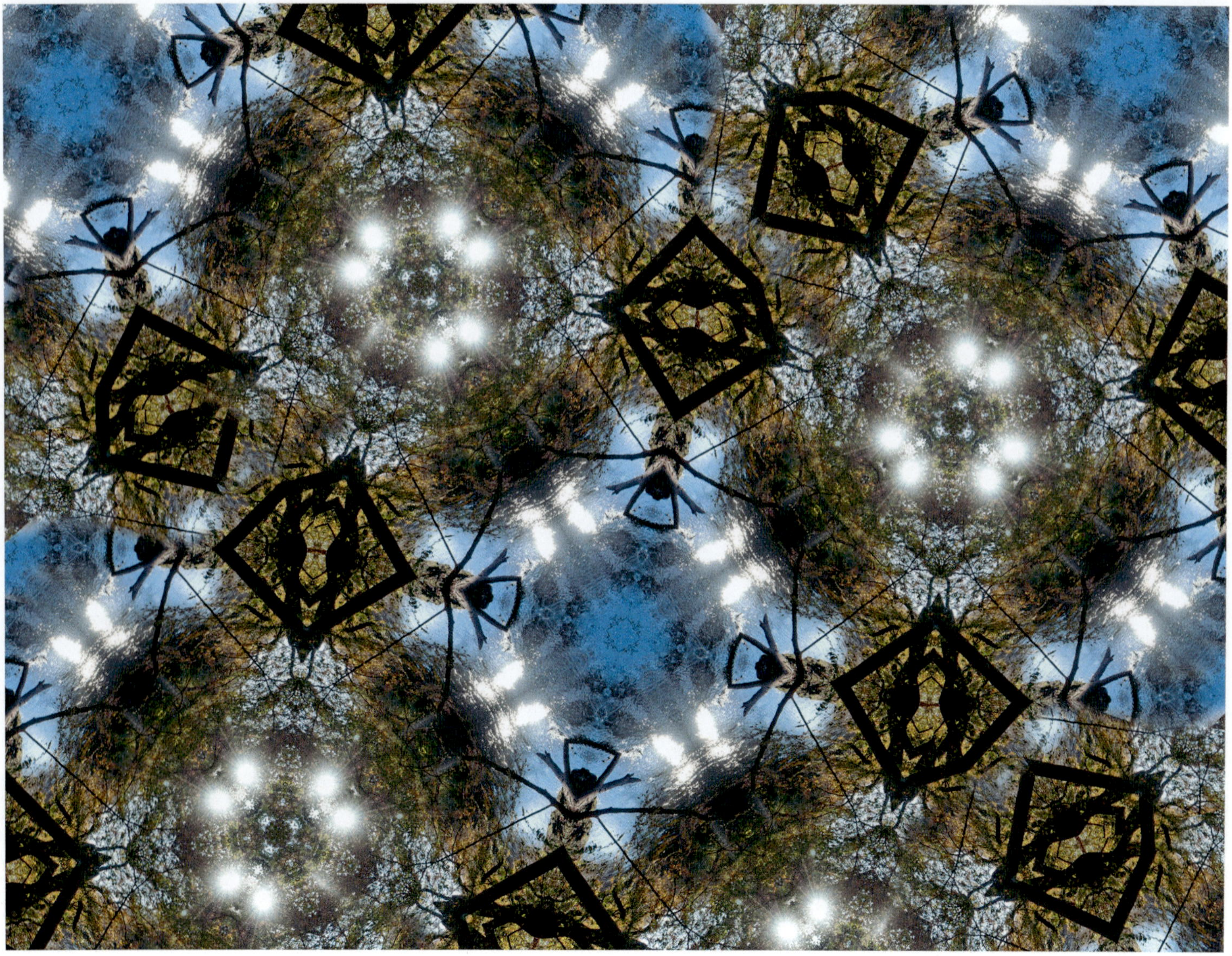

Acknowledgments

I acknowledge...

Dr. Glenda D. Goss, for providing an invaluable sounding board throughout the creative process.

I acknowledge...

Dr. Glenda and Angela Goss for joining me on the Bartram Trail in Florida.

I acknowledge...

Dr. James W. Thompson, for his support and for joining me on the Bartram Canoe Trail in Alabama.

I acknowledge...

Heather Gladfelter for all the Franklin Tree Adventures she has invited me on, leading me to photograph the *Franklinia alatmaha* in bloom.

I acknowledge...

My network of friends who have been an invaluable resource sustaining me emotionally and mentally throughout the creative process.

I acknowledge...

You, for being an intrepid explorer of these worlds of the Southeastern United States: Cities, Creatures, Plants, and Waters.

72485686R00064

Made in the USA
Columbia, SC
01 September 2019